First Facts®

Benjamin Banneker

SELF-EDUCATED SCIENTIST

by Lisa M. Bolt Simons

CAPSTONE PRESS
a capstone imprint

First Facts are published by Capstone Press,
1710 Roe Crest Drive, North Mankato, Minnesota 56003
www.mycapstone.com

Library of Congress Cataloging-in-Publication Data:
Library of Congress Cataloging-in-Publication Data is available on the Library of
Congress website.
ISBN: 978-1-5435-0645-7 (library binding) -- 978-1-5435-0651-8 (paperback) --
978-1-5435-0657-0 (ebook)
Summary: This book presents the life of Benjamin Banneker, the self-educated scientist
who helped plan our nation's capital city.

Editorial Credits
Anna Butzer, editor; Bobbie Nuytten, designer;
Jo Miller, media researcher; Laura Manthe, production specialist

Photo Credits
Alamy: MPVHistory, 21, Paul Fearn, cover; Bridgeman Images: Private Collection/
Migratory Locust, 17; Getty Images: Stock Montage/Contributor, 7; Library of Congress,
Prints and Photographs Division, 15, 19; North Wind Picture Archives, 9; Shutterstock:
Rudenkois, 11, siloto, cover (background);The George F. Landegger Collection of
District of Columbia Photographs in Carol M. Highsmith's America, Library of
Congress, Prints and Photographs Division, 5; The Image Works: TopFoto, 13

Design Elements
Shutterstock: siloto

Printed in the United States of America.
010868S18

Table of Contents

CHAPTER 1

Saving the Nation's Capital

In 1789 the person hired to design our nation's capital city quit. He took all the plans with him. Benjamin Banneker had seen the plans. He had an excellent memory. He recreated the plans in two days. Benjamin helped save the Washington, D.C., we know today.

FACT Thomas Jefferson asked Benjamin to help with the plans for the capital. Jefferson later became the third U.S. president.

ALMANAC

CHAPTER 2

A Natural

Benjamin Banneker was born November 9, 1731, in Ellicott's Mills, Maryland. His mother, Mary, was from England. His father, Robert, was a freed slave. Benjamin grew up in Baltimore County. About 200 free African Americans, 4,000 slaves, and 13,000 Caucasians lived in this area.

Finding Freedom

Slavery was legal in Maryland until 1864. Some slaves could buy their freedom from their owners. Others escaped. Benjamin's father was born a slave. His owner later freed him.

Portrait of Benjamin Banneker

Benjamin's grandmother taught him to read and write. Benjamin also went to a **Quaker** school. All races were allowed in the school. This was unusual for the time. Benjamin did very well in both math and science.

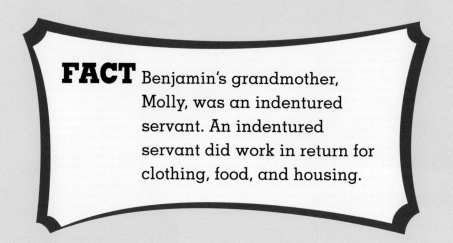

FACT Benjamin's grandmother, Molly, was an indentured servant. An indentured servant did work in return for clothing, food, and housing.

Quaker—founded in the 1600s, a group of people known as the Religious Society of Friends who opposed war

A Quaker schoolhouse

"The color of the skin is in no way connected with strength of the mind or intellectual powers."

Benjamin Banneker

In 1751 Benjamin took apart a pocket watch. He drew the pieces. He studied how they worked. Then he carved the pieces and built a wooden clock. It took him two years. It was the first time an American made a clock out of only wood. Benjamin's clock worked for 50 years.

Pieces of a pocket watch

Later in life Benjamin became friends with the Ellicott brothers. He borrowed tools and books from them. Benjamin studied **astronomy** books. He was almost able to **predict** a **solar eclipse**. A mistake was in his sources, not his math. In 1789 Benjamin recreated the capital plans. Two years later he worked with an Ellicott relative to **survey** the nation's capital.

astronomy—the study of stars, planets, and other objects in space

predict—to say what you think will happen in the future

solar eclipse—a period of daytime darkness when the moon passes between the sun and earth

survey—to determine the size, shape, location, and other details about land

Benjamin Banneker and Andrew Ellicott surveying Washington, D.C.

The Ellicott Family Business

The Ellicott family owned a gristmill. This mill had water wheels that turned millstones. The millstones ground grain into flour.

CHAPTER 3

Almanac Author

In 1792 Benjamin **published** an **almanac**. In the book he predicted positions for the sun, moon, and planets. Benjamin used math to make these predictions. Farmers used information from the book. It helped them decide when to plant and harvest. Sailors used the book too. It helped them to **forecast** the ocean tides.

publish—to produce and distribute a book, magazine, newspaper, or any other printed material so that people can buy it

almanac—a yearly magazine or book that contains facts and information

forecast—making a prediction using science and math

Title page of Benjamin's Almanac published in 1792

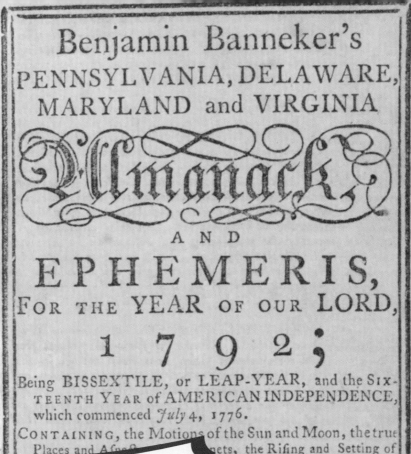

Benjamin Banneker's PENNSYLVANIA, DELAWARE, MARYLAND and VIRGINIA Almanack AND EPHEMERIS, FOR THE YEAR OF OUR LORD, 1792; Being BISSEXTILE, or LEAP-YEAR, and the SIXTEENTH YEAR of AMERICAN INDEPENDENCE, which commenced July 4, 1776. CONTAINING, the Motions of the Sun and Moon, the true Places and Ages ... ets, the Rifing and Setting of ... ng and Southing, Place and Age ... ations, Conjunctions, Eclipfes, ... Festivals, and other remarkable ... Supreme and Circuit Courts of the ... ual Courts in Pennsylvania, Dela- ... nia.—Also, several useful Tables, ... arious Selections from the Com- ... ucky Philosopher, an American Sage; ... ning Essays, in Profe and Verfe— ... er, more pleasing, and useful Va- ... Kind and Price in North-America.

BALTIMORE: Printed and Sold, Wholesale and Retail, by WILLIAM GODDARD and JAMES ANGELL, at their Printing-Office, in Market-Street.—Sold, alfo, by Mr. JOSEPH CRUKSHANK, Printer, in Market-Street, and Mr. DANIEL HUMPHREYS, Printer, in South-Front-Street, Philadelphia—and by Meffrs. HANSON and BOND, Printers, in Alexandria

FACT Benjamin designed a farm that grew wheat. The wheat helped U.S. soldiers fight hunger during the Revolutionary War (1775–1783).

Benjamin also wrote poems and essays. He included them in his almanacs. He published six almanacs from 1792 to 1797. Books were not common in homes at the time. Sales slowed down. Benjamin stopped publishing the books.

FACT Benjamin also studied bees and **locusts**. He did not put the information in his almanacs. He just enjoyed the science.

locusts—an insect related to the grasshopper that can destroy farmland in large numbers

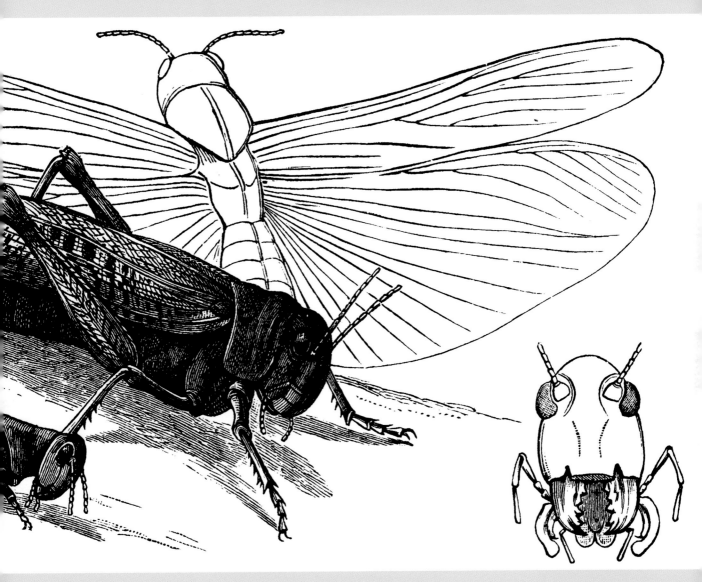

CHAPTER 4

Outspoken about Equal Rights

Benjamin sent his 1792 almanac and a letter to Thomas Jefferson. He told Jefferson that **prejudice** against African Americans should stop. Jefferson agreed but didn't make any changes. Benjamin kept fighting for equal rights.

prejudice—hatred or unfair treatment of people who belong to a certain social group, such as a race or religion

A letter dated August 30, 1791, from Thomas Jefferson to Benjamin.

FACT Benjamin put his letter and Jefferson's response in the 1793 almanac.

Benjamin died October 9, 1806. He was 74 years old. The day of his funeral, his house burned down. Inside was the wooden clock he built 50 years earlier. The clock was just one part of Benjamin's **legacy** as a scientist and inventor.

"Never abandon your vision. Keep reaching to further your dream."

Benjamin Banneker

legacy—qualities and actions that one is remembered for

Glossary

almanac (AWL-muh-nak)—a yearly magazine or book that contains facts and information

astronomy (uh-STRAH-nuh-mee)—the study of stars, planets, and other objects in space

forecast (FOR-kast)—a report of future weather conditions

legacy (LEG-uh-see)—qualities and actions that one is remembered for

locust (loh-KUST)—an insect related to the grasshopper that can destroy farmland in large numbers

predict (pri-DIKT)—to say what you think will happen in the future

prejudice (PREJ-uh-diss)—hatred or unfair treatment of people who belong to a certain social group

publish (PUHB-lish)— to produce and distribute a book or any other printed material so that people can buy it

Quaker (KWAY-kur)—founded in the 1600s, a group of people known as the Religious Society of Friends who opposed war

solar eclipse (SOH-lur i-KLIPSS)—a period of daytime darkness when the moon passes between the sun and earth

survey (SUR-vay)—to determine the size, shape, location, and other details about land

Read More

Keller, Shana. *Ticktock Banneker's Clock*. Ann Arbor, Mich.: Sleeping Bear Press, 2016.

Martin, Isabel. *Benjamin Banneker*. North Mankato, Minn.: Capstone Press, 2015.

Wittekind, Erika. *Benjamin Banneker: Brilliant Surveyor, Mathematician, and Astronomer*. Minneapolis: ABDO Publishing Company, 2015.

Internet Sites

Use Facthound to find Internet sites related to this book.

Visit *www.facthound.com*

Just type in 9781543506457 and go!

Check out projects, games and lots more at
www.capstonekids.com

Critical Thinking Questions

1. In what ways was Benjamin intelligent? Find examples from the text.

2. Why were almanacs so important to farmers and sailors during Benjamin's lifetime?

Index